MW01131444

AWESOME DOGS

Vizslas

by Kaitlyn Duling

BLASTOFF!
2
READERS

BELLWETHER MEDIA • MINNEAPOLIS, MN

Note to Librarians, Teachers, and Parents:

Blastoff! Readers are carefully developed by literacy experts and combine standards-based content with developmentally appropriate text.

Level 1 provides the most support through repetition of high-frequency words, light text, predictable sentence patterns, and strong visual support.

Level 2 offers early readers a bit more challenge through varied simple sentences, increased text load, and less repetition of high-frequency words.

Level 3 advances early-fluent readers toward fluency through increased text and concept load, less reliance on visuals, longer sentences, and more literary language.

Level 4 builds reading stamina by providing more text per page, increased use of punctuation, greater variation in sentence patterns, and increasingly challenging vocabulary.

Level 5 encourages children to move from "learning to read" to "reading to learn" by providing even more text, varied writing styles, and less familiar topics.

Whichever book is right for your reader, Blastoff! Readers are the perfect books to build confidence and encourage a love of reading that will last a lifetime!

This edition first published in 2020 by Bellwether Media, Inc.

No part of this publication may be reproduced in whole or in part without written permission of the publisher. For information regarding permission, write to Bellwether Media, Inc., Attention: Permissions Department, 6012 Blue Circle Drive, Minnetonka, MN 55343.

Library of Congress Cataloging-in-Publication Data

Names: Duling, Kaitlyn, author.
Title: Vizslas / by Kaitlyn Duling.
Description: Minneapolis, MN : Bellwether Media, Inc., [2020] |
    Series: Blastoff! readers: awesome dogs | Includes bibliographical references and index. | Audience: Ages 5-8 |
    Audience: Grades K-1 | Summary: "Relevant images match informative text in this introduction to Vizslas.
    Intended for students in kindergarten through third grade"– Provided by publisher.
Identifiers: LCCN 2019024246 (print) | LCCN 2019024247 (ebook) |
    ISBN 9781644871188 (library binding) | ISBN 9781618917683 (ebook)
Subjects: LCSH: Vizsla–Juvenile literature.
Classification: LCC SF429.V5 D85 2020 (print) | LCC SF429.V5 (ebook) | DDC 636.752–dc23
LC record available at https://lccn.loc.gov/2019024246
LC ebook record available at https://lccn.loc.gov/2019024247

Editor: Rebecca Sabelko   Designer: Laura Sowers

Printed in the United States of America, North Mankato, MN.

Table of Contents

What Are Vizslas?

Vizslas are smart, active dogs. They are built to hunt and play!

Vizslas are also loving.
They care for their families!

Vizslas have sweet, friendly faces. Their eyes and noses match their **coats**.

Long, floppy ears frame their cheeks.

These dogs love to run. Long, **lean** legs help them go fast.

Vizslas are a medium-sized **breed**. They weigh up to 60 pounds (27 kilograms).

Vizslas have smooth, thick coats. Their hair is short.

Vizsla Coats

rust   golden

Most vizslas have **rust** coats. Others are a lighter, golden color. Both coat colors may have white markings.

History of Vizslas

Vizslas come from Hungary.
Many worked for **nobles**.

Hungary

N W E S

They hunted birds and small animals. Later, they delivered messages during World War I.

Vizslas joined the **American Kennel Club** in 1960. They are in the **Sporting Group**.

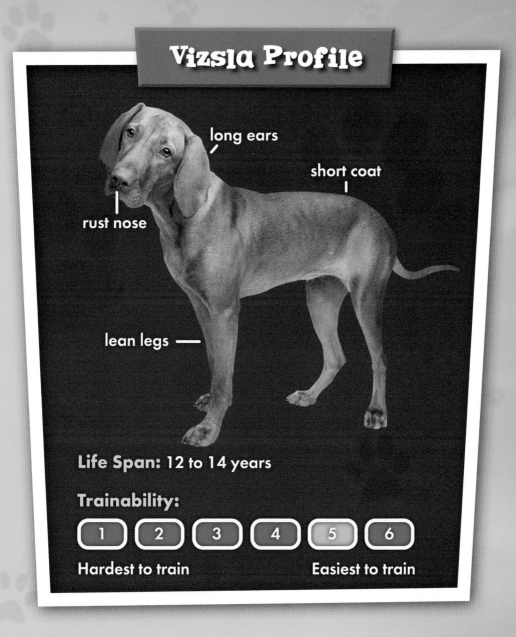

Vizsla Profile

long ears

short coat

rust nose

lean legs —

Life Span: 12 to 14 years

Trainability:

1	2	3	4	5	6

Hardest to train   Easiest to train

Since then, vizslas have done special jobs like **search and rescue**. They helped after the **9/11 attacks**.

Exercise is fun with vizslas. They keep up with runners and bikers.

They also enjoy games and **obedience** training.

Vizlas are hard workers that are up for any job!

They make excellent **guide dogs**.
They can also be **therapy dogs**.

Vizslas are often called "Velcro vizslas" because they love to be near people.

These dogs are great
furry friends!

Glossary

9/11 attacks—a series of four attacks against the United States that occurred on September 11, 2001

American Kennel Club—an organization that keeps track of dog breeds in the United States

breed—a type of dog

coats—the hair or fur covering some animals

guide dogs—dogs trained to help people who are blind perform everyday tasks

lean—thin

nobles—members of the upper class

obedience—related to following rules

rust—reddish-brown color

search and rescue—teams that look for and help people in danger

Sporting Group—a group of dog breeds that are active and need regular exercise

therapy dogs—dogs that comfort people who are sick, hurt, or have a disability

To Learn More

AT THE LIBRARY

Mills, Andrea. *The Everything Book of Dogs and Puppies.* New York, N.Y.: DK, 2018.

Resler, T.J. *Dog Breed Guide.* Washington, D.C.: National Geographic Kids, 2019.

Shaffer, Lindsay. *Brittanys.* Minneapolis, Minn.: Bellwether Media, 2019.

ON THE WEB

FACTSURFER

Factsurfer.com gives you a safe, fun way to find more information.

1. Go to www.factsurfer.com.

2. Enter "vizslas" into the search box and click 🔍.

3. Select your book cover to see a list of related web sites.

Index

The images in this book are reproduced through the courtesy of: Ivonne Wierink, front cover; Ivanova N, pp. 4-5, 6-7, 8, 10-11, 16-17; Csanad Kiss, pp. 5, 11 (right); Fenne, p. 7; Aneta Jungerova, pp. 8-9; kristiillustra, p. 11 (left); Sproetniek, p. 12; Daniel Dempster Photography/ Alamy, p. 13; Osetrik, p. 14; Erik Lam, p. 15; Zenotri, p. 17; jszs19, p. 18; The Washington Post/ Getty, pp. 18-19; National Geographic Image Collection/ Alamy, p. 20; Janet Horton/ Alamy, p. 21.